DEAR OLD LOVE

Anonymous Notes to Former Crushes,
Sweethearts, Husbands, Wives
& Ones That Got Away

....

COMPILED AND EDITED BY
ANDY SELSBERG

....

WORKMAN PUBLISHING • NEW YORK

Library of Congress Cataloging-in-Publication Data
is available.

ISBN 978-0-7611-5605-5

Workman books are available at special discounts
when purchased in bulk for premiums and sales
promotions as well as for fund-raising or educational
use. Special editions or book excerpts can also be
created to specification. For details, contact the
Special Sales Director at the address below.

Cover design by Robb Allen
Interior design by Diana Zantopp

Hand with Quill Pen, Courtesy of the
New York State Museum, Albany, N.Y. 12230.
Inkwell © Veer

Workman Publishing Company, Inc.
225 Varick Street
New York, NY 10014-4381
www.workman.com

Printed in China

First printing September 2009

10 9 8 7 6 5 4 3 2 1

INTRODUCTION

I got married recently. Commitment can be
fun, but all our connections to past loves
don't evaporate upon taking a vow. Part of
me is still fifteen, riding go-carts with a girl
I wanted to kiss. I continue to berate myself
for moments in relationships when I should
have been more considerate—deodorant for
her birthday? Idiot! And I'll wonder: Is there
a statute of limitations on flowers? Here I am
in the shower, trying to finish off quarrels
that ended years ago. Or, I'll picture someone
I admired, and think how we could've had a
fiery affair, if only I'd spoken up. I rue times
when I didn't kiss back, times when I didn't
appreciate what I was getting, times when
she didn't appreciate what I was giving.

As a way to settle into marriage, I wanted
to reconcile all this extra desire, fondness,
anger, and regret. I can't sing or play guitar,
and direct communication is too sticky and
impractical, if not impossible. I needed a

bottle for all this, and a sea to throw it into: out there, but not headed anywhere. Luckily, that's what the Internet is for. And I figured if I had a bunch of old love business to take care of, the rest of the world would too, so I started the Dear Old Love project.

Dear Old Love began as a website: dearoldlove.com. There, people can send messages to former flames and objects of affection—all anonymously. I edit and post what I think are the funniest, the saddest, the sweetest, the smartest, the most illuminating, and, sometimes, the most spiteful. A good Dear Old Love note is the long, sloppy story of a heart, condensed to a line.

In the future there may be many more arms to the Dear Old Love project: coffee mugs, pinball machines, charter schools, a perfume that smells like a breakup conversation in an autumn garden. But for now we'll start with a book—this book—which is what I envisioned from the beginning. A book because ruminations on love are best digested at the speed of literature, with ink on paper. A book because you can't really *give* someone a website: "Happy anniversary, darling. Check out this link!" And a book because the best books are beguiling and enduring, like memories of our best and dearest old loves.

Here we are reaching out to the ones that got away, and the ones we held onto for years. This is a collection of notes from the world, to the world. And they all begin, "Dear Old Love . . ."

—Andy Selsberg

Dear Old Love . . .

HAPPY ENDING

I'm so glad it didn't work out the way I wanted it to.

ADVICE

Mother told me, "Don't buy the first coat you try on." So I broke up with you. But in retrospect, I think she was talking about coats.
Sorry.

PELTED

I'm consoled by the fact that the two of you will have very hairy children.

IT'S NOT YOU
*Yes, we had good sex.
I have good sex with everyone.
That's me.*

BLUE RULES
*Putting ketchup in a bowl, no
drinking from cans because you'll cut
your lip, special slippers for guests.
Being at your mom's house was like
those crazy laws from the 1800s that
say you can't walk a duck on a leash
in Pennsylvania.*

BIG SOLO
*When I play air guitar,
you're my air audience.*

BOWLED OVER

I can't believe I miss hearing you yell "Now that's what I'm talking about!" after bowel movements you were particularly proud of.

U OF YOU

You were the only worthwhile thing I studied in college.

TONIGHT'S SPECIAL

I never tired of looking at you over the tops of menus.

DOPPIO

*Since you left, I still make two
cups of coffee in the morning.
I drink both of them.*

FLAKE

*I'm dreading the first snowfall,
because I'll have to remember a
Sunday, white sheets, and pillow
creases on your face.*

XMAS

*The earrings were nice.
But what I really wanted
was an orgasm.*

HEY BABY

If all I cared about was producing a genetic masterpiece, I would've stayed with you.

LAB WORK

You taught me how long I can handle a relationship based solely on sexual chemistry. Seven months.

SHHHH

I would have been happy with our secret love affair forever. We could have secretly moved to California and had secret jobs on a secret vineyard.

LOVE IN THE TIME OF LUNESTA
They set us up because we both have trouble sleeping. That should have been a sign.

PET PEEVED

I don't care that you miss my dog. When you cheated on me, you cheated on him, too.

GO BALD ALREADY
I hate the idea of you keeping all your hair and me not being able to touch it whenever I want.

CLASS NOTES
You should publish an alumni newsletter for everyone you've dated. I'd like to see what my colleagues are up to. We're a good group.

MISSING MISS
Your maiden name lives on hard in my fantasy world.

MRS. HIM

I still use your last name when I doodle my future signature.

IS THIS YOUR FLOOR?

I smelled your perfume on an elevator and it took me back ten years. An old woman dressed like a teenager was wearing it.

MEGAPIXEL REGRET

I wish we'd invested in a better camera. And used it.

UNSUBSCRIBED

A woman called for you yesterday. I started to tell her off, but she was just selling subscriptions to The Chronicle.

SO CLOSE BUT YET

*Why are you my best friend,
and not my best husband?*

MAGINOT LINING

*Remember in tenth grade
when I said we should meet
at Victoria's Secret, and you
showed up with your friends?
I was giving you a visa to the
land of adult sexuality, and
you tried to smuggle three
doofuses across the border.*

OVERBLOWN

You blew me all out of proportion.

LUCKY STRIKE

I have to believe our relationship continues to play out in all those particles of cigarette smoke we exhaled together.

REST IN PEACE

I always preferred your pillow. Now that it's mine I don't like it so much.

RIBBED

I wish we'd been close enough for you to go on the pill.

TIED UP

*Your penchant for neck scarves
makes me want to autoerotically
asphyxiate myself by way of tribute.*

MOMENT OF CLARITIN

*I discovered the hard
way that I'm allergic to
your cat, your laundry
detergent, and your
deepest beliefs.*

PAGING MR. SNOTBORG

*I let you go because I couldn't stand
your last name.*

IN MY LEAGUE, BRIEFLY

*Your laughter was music.
Your eyes were jewels.
Even your farts smelled like
Shalimar. Thank you for
rebounding off me.*

◆

IDIOCRACY

*I still say you're an idiot for
not falling in love with me.*

◆

MEASUREMENT

*Even though we broke up five years
ago, I still rate the way I feel about
someone new on a scale that goes
from Zero to You.*

CLASSIFIED

*I ran that Missed Connection
notice looking for you for so long
it became a regular feature,
like those beret ads in the back
of* The New Yorker.

TRADING DOWN

*You gave the impression that being
with me was settling, which I was
fine with, but then you didn't settle.*

SHAKE

*I could only get so stoned on
the stems, seeds, and resin
of your affection.*

LAMENT
It's so hard to cyberstalk a technophobe.

BALANCE
I do not miss your drunken rages. I do not miss paying for everything. I absolutely do not miss your insane family, and I do not miss uncovering your many lies. However, I think of you often while masturbating.

TOUGH JOB
Every morning my boss asks if I'm all right. Every morning I lie.

1 - 2 - 3 - 4 - 5

Please change your e-mail password. I'm addicted.

DRESS CODE

*You taught me: If he dresses
like a douchebag,
he's probably a douchebag.*

ONE NOTE

*I stopped talking to everyone who grew
tired of hearing me talk about you.
So now I don't really talk to anyone.*

TOUCHDOWN
I root for the Giants because of you.
My husband has no idea.

———◆———

IS THIS THING ON?
I realized later on that our blowjob-
centric sex belied deep issues about
your experiences with intercourse.
You were telling me you had problems
and I didn't listen, even though you
were speaking right into the mic.

———◆———

AS GOOD AS I GET
You made me want
to be a lesser man.

COME BACK KID
Come back from Tanzania.
I want to get a cabin in a ski town
and have babies with you.

———◆———

LOCATION, LOCATION, RELATION

I could live in the
same small town
my whole life if you
were there, too.

———◆———

REMEMBER HOMEROOM!
You signed my ninth grade
yearbook, "We could've used a
girl like you at the Alamo."
I've had a thing for you ever since.

SOUR INVESTMENT
*You operated an emotional Ponzi
scheme with many, many women,
and I was the last to cash out.*

NUMBERS GAME
I'm glad you were my fourth.

WUV BITES
*You thought the way I pronounced
certain words was cute. Now I feel like
I have a speech impediment.*

BLESS YOU
*I'm still searching for someone
with a stranger and more endearing
sneeze than yours.*

MINUS ONE
I'm still in love with you, and you're in love with every woman except me.

SCOTCHED
I was afraid if you got close, you'd see the Scotch tape holding me together.

UNHAPPY ENDING
Then again, if you hadn't been a full-service masseuse, we never would have met in the first place.

JUST FOR LUCK

I wish I'd saved a few pairs of your underwear, to seal in a jar and keep on a shelf high in the pantry. Is that the sort of thing that makes you miss me, or glad it's over?

SCRATCH THAT

If I'd known I was only going to get one shot, I would have left more marks.

E-LOVE BUT NOT *IN* LOVE

"I love you" doesn't count if you can only say it in e-mail.

SNOW LEOPARD IS NEXT
When I said you were the only boy I called Puppy, I lied. I'd been calling my boyfriends that since high school. I feel so guilty about it that I've switched to Tiger.

SPELLING CUMULUS WITHOUT US
You made all the clouds look sad.

HELLO DARKNESS MY OLD FRIEND
I held out hope that you'd come rushing into the temple, tear down the chuppah, and declare your love for me right up until the moment I smashed the glass.

EVEN I GET THE BLUES
I kept all your Tom Robbins books.

FORCING IT
Ours was an Obi-Wan relationship.
We struck it down, but then it
became more powerful than we
could possibly imagine.

AT MY MIDDLE

You never saw me
at my best. Now I'm
worried that maybe
there is no such thing.

TELL ME MORE
I love how you always chewed gum when we had sex. It was like doing it with a '50s carhop.

WAS I WRONG? DEPENDS.
Because your father vowed to do everything in his power to break us up, and he did, I enrolled him in NAMBLA and flooded his mailbox with hairpiece catalogs and coupons for adult diapers.

LOST AND FOUND
I miss flea-marketing with you. You had a way of turning old junk into slightly less junky junk.

BEAUTY SCHOOL DROPOUT
*I'm sorry I didn't trust you
to cut my hair.*

◆

CAMP SWEETHEART
*I know you only gave me a
backrub because you happened
to be standing behind me when
the music stopped, but to me,
at fourteen, it felt like fate.*

◆

LINKED IN
*I held onto the jade cufflinks you gave
me for the prom, forty-nine years ago.
I just gave them to my son.*

BETTER LOVING
THROUGH METAPHOR

Dear Old Love,
Our relationship was like . . .

- my singing voice—way better in my head.

- a jam band. It went on far too long and only made sense on drugs. Fun at the time, though.

- a thriller that you can never read again because you already know the grisly ending.

- a perfect pair of jeans that gets irreversibly cut off at the knees one hot summer day.

- a great song that gets played so often you can no longer hear what made it great.

- the idea for a National Service Corps—way too much personal sacrifice involved.

- an inflatable guest bed—handy to have around, but yielded mostly restless nights.

- single-malt scotch. Now, I could appreciate it.

- a coin-op ride outside the supermarket—underwhelming and vaguely sticky. But still, the world would be sadder without it.

- Times Square—better when it was worse.

- a fireplace video. It crackled, and looked convincing, but provided no actual warmth.

- a Rubik's Cube. I smashed it on the ground so I wouldn't waste any more time with it.

- an old episode of *Seinfeld*. I can't imagine a late night where I wouldn't be happy to revisit it for 22 minutes.

- a possible no-hitter. We were obliged not to mention the lack of scoring until it was over.

- a banned insecticide. It worked amazingly well, but probably would have killed us.

- the core of a star—too hot not to cool down.

RUN BACK

If only I'd thought to bottle the way your neck smelled after a jog along the river.

SWITCHEROO

I have replaced you with a body pillow.

SILVER FOX

Couldn't you just consolidate and work off your credit card debt instead of going to Belize with that old man?

WHY MATTERS
*I think you came back because I asked
you, not because you wanted to.*

**MY MISTRESS' EYES ARE
NOTHING LIKE THE SUN**
*You are assless and have stick-out
ribs, but you are tubby, too.
You've read Proust in French
but live in West Texas. You think a
lot about clothes but wear pajamas
most of the time. Your feet smell
awful. All of this I loved.*

WRAPPED
*My love for you is like a
mummy—carefully preserved,
with the brains yanked out.*

UNPRECEDENTED

*When we first got together and you
asked how many women I'd slept
with, I thought you were worried
about STDs. Now I'm pretty sure
it was my sexual technique
that made you ask.*

CAN YOU HEAR ME NOW?

*I've gone through three phones since
we last spoke. How many more before
I stop transferring your number?*

SOHO SAD

*I was there for those first paintings,
and now I don't get to go to
your openings.*

MISSED SOME SPOTS

Wish I could've saved some of your freckles, somehow.

BEEN BAD

You turned and said, "Spank me. I give you permission." But I couldn't bring myself to hurt you. I sure would like to take you up on it now, though.

IN THE FOLD

I still make those paper cranes and dollar bill rings you showed me. For my daughters.

APPLE OF MINE
*I was more than ready to give
you a shot, but I could never be
with someone who considers
chucking an apple core an
unforgivable act of littering.*

HOW'S SPOT?
*When I see you, what I really want
to ask about is your vagina. It'd be
like asking about a beloved dog.
"How's the vagina? What's it up to?
Any adorable mischief lately?
Give it a pat for me!"*

FAIR TRADE
*You broke my heart, but refined my
grammar and sense of style.*

DAY OFF
*Could we take a one-day vacation
from our lives and spend it wandering
around an old amusement park at
the edge of summer?*

DOWNTURN

I should've hoarded you for the lean times.

EYE-TALIAN
*I resent it when people
compliment the glasses you got
for me in Milan, because it's
like they're praising you.
But I do look great in them.*

HEMLINING

I regret not being able to see you dressed in all the fashions that have come and gone since we split.

LET'S HEAR IT FOR HALFWAY

It's okay that we never made it to the top.

MAY DAY

Five-foot-nothing. Thirty-seven. Red hair past your ass. Five cats. White convertible with overdue payments. Unblended lipliner. Playboy tattoo. Day tripper. You had more red flags than Mother Russia.

ROCKY ROAD

*I got fat after we broke up,
but don't let that swell your head.
It was more because I was working
at the ice cream store.*

WILLIAM'S PENN

*When I get a hard-on,
it points towards
Philadelphia. It thinks
you're still there.*

FIFTEEN MINUTES OF LAME

*You left me for someone who doesn't
know who Andy Warhol is.*

SQUASHED

We would have stayed together longer if you weren't such a militant vegan. But I will always remember the summer when I ate only sides. By August I saw you as a talking pork chop.

ITTIGI LITTIGUV YITTIGOU

Thank you for teaching me how to say "I love you" in gibberish.

THE COUPLE THAT HATES TOGETHER

We had contempt for all the same things and people, and I still can't believe that that wasn't enough.

SHOELESS JILL
In my book, being the Girl Who Walked Around Campus Barefoot means you'll always be a celebrity worthy of desire, even if you've long since shod yourself.

OPPOSITE DAYS
*For the record:
I hate you = I love you.
I said it a lot. I still do.
Hate you.*

FINAL TALLY
You are the only person I ever enjoyed kissing.

AFTER FONDUE

It was a miracle that we ended up in a private room at that hostel in Paris. I'm still sad I was too shy to crawl into your bed because you kept talking about your boyfriend back home. Boyfriend? We were 20! In Paris!

KAME-KAME-HA

I miss the ninja yells while you tickled me to tears.

TYPIST

I hate when people ask me what my "type" is. Because I always end up describing you.

BOYS MATURE SLOWER
*I needed ten years to
catch up with you.*

EXTRA, EXTRA
My Times *subscription is still
in your name. Either you never look
at your credit card statement, or you
want to stay in my life by providing
me with a hard copy of the news.*

GRADE A

*You are a gigantic ass.
And not the good
kind of gigantic ass,
like my ass.*

HEY LADYSMITH

*I thought your "sixy" South African
accent made up for the extra weight,
but try telling that to my friends.*

LATE FEE

*I asked for my DVDs back,
but what I really wanted
was for you to return all the
love I gave you.*

CHICAGO HOPELESS

*I accept the fact that I supported
you through medical school. I don't
think it's wrong of me to expect
free health advice and prescriptions
on demand for life.*

STYLE POINTS

I keep trying to get my hair back to exactly the way it was when you loved me.

MARLBORO FIGHTS

I thought it was sweet the way you smoked a pack every time we had a big argument.

CYBER SUMMARY

Online: you were perfect.
Then: disaster.

I'VE TRIED
*All this would be so much easier
if I hated you.*

ALL ABOUT YU
*I studied enough Italian to have
conversations with your parents,
but you only learned enough
Cantonese to count to ten.*

NO-NAME DROPPING
*I still talk about you
all the time. You're my
brilliant, nameless
"friend."*

PABLO, HONEY

I practice Borges and Neruda aloud
so I can read them to you in the
mother tongue someday.

PSYCHIATRIC HELP 5¢

It's nice you went
to therapy after we
broke up. I wish you'd
gone while we were
still together.

THE NOTHINGTON POST

Found your secret blog.
It's so boring!

NOTHING GOLDSCHLÄGER CAN STAY
I was drunker than I'd ever been.
You tasted like cinnamon.
Is your name really Paco?
Because no one believes me.

HERSUTE
I hope you didn't go through those
hair-removal procedures for me.
I like my women mammals.

KILLJOY
How were you against
holding hands? That's like
hating springtime, or
being anti-kitten.

THE REAL DEAL

I'm sorry I accused you of pretending to be gay.

◆

WINONA AND FRIENDS FOREVER

I don't regret getting a tattoo of your name. I just watered it down by adding a bunch of other lovers.

◆

HAVAIANAS NIGHTS

Your shoes were terrible; I wish we'd dated during flip-flop season.

A MORE CIVILIZED AGE
It both cheers and saddens me
to think that glow-in-the-dark
condoms plus lightsaber sound
effects comprised the high point
of our relationship.

NEAR MISS
I wish I missed you,
so I could do that instead
of just feeling empty.

GO FIGARO
Thanks to the tragedy of our breakup,
I now love opera. But I can't find
anyone who will go with me.

NO VIBRATIONS

It kills me that we were too young, shy, and oblivious to use toys.

FUN SCALE

Being with you was fun, but fantasizing about you is funner.

OLD STYLE

I started collecting vintage erotica because they have bodies and hair like yours.

WELL, DUH
I miss that stupid face
you made during sex.

I, SPECTATOR

I may have exaggerated my devotion to sports to win you, but my love of sitting, eating, and watching things was genuine.

MULLIGAN
Can I have a do-over?

CURSES

*You couldn't dress up like an elf
and pretend I was a wizard
that cast a sex spell on you?
You are not a dreamer like me.*

◆

TIMING MACHINE

*I wish we'd met when
we were sixteen.*

◆

FRESHEN UP

*Do me this favor. Next time you're
in bed with a girl you're not
serious about, and she says she'll
be right back from the bathroom,
don't whisper, "I'll miss you."*

THE REAL ENDING

Dear Old Love,
I knew it was over when . . .

- the back rubs tapered off to one every three years.

- you got back into the car with all that beef jerky.

- you used the recession as an excuse to stop going to the movies.

- you said the secret to a long marriage was freedom.

- you got the call about your father. I'm not good with bad times.

- you started secretly making copies of my recipes.

- you claimed to have outgrown dirty limericks.

- you no longer looked me in the eyes on video chat.

- you quit straining the pulp from my orange juice.

- I saw his silver Audi in front of your place. Good-bye, and thanks for slumming.

- you gave up cunnilingus for Lent.

- your mom yelled at me for not knowing who Rebecca from the Bible was. With the way she was talking I thought this Rebecca was a neighbor of yours.

- you had a second kid. Through marriage and kid #1, I figured I still had a shot.

- you stopped being real and started being polite.

- I started living vicariously through your infidelities.

- you didn't pay for my dinner. For the two-hundred-and-fiftieth time.

- you stopped hoisting me up onto your shoulders at outdoor concerts. And, we stopped going to concerts.

- you quit wanting to coordinate our Halloween costumes.

- you wept and said you no longer loved me.

SLEAZE LIKE US

Crawl back into the hole you came out of. And take me with you.

BOOK HIM
*I finally finished my novel.
It's nothing like the early drafts you read. The character based on you kills himself because he's a jackass and everybody hates him. Especially me.*

LOW FIDELITY
I put on the mixes you made for me just to hear everyone complain about how terrible they are.

DARN IT
You like the club scene. I like to knit.
You said that wouldn't matter. It did.

INDECENT PROPOSAL
I didn't want to say yes.
It's just that it's very hard to say
no when someone whips out a
ring on top of Table Mountain
and his family is at the bottom
waiting to celebrate the
"good news."

AN AMERICAN CLASSIC
I liked your roommate better.

PRETTY COLD, HUH?

I had so much small talk prepared for when I saw you, but when you appeared, I couldn't say anything.

WILD WEST

When I think about you living alone in that cabin, I ache to bring you coffee, a horse, and a fiddle.

CAST IRONY

I left because you threw the frying pan at my head, and now the thing I miss most is your cheesy eggs.

NATIONAL GEOGRAPHIC

Inverted nipple canyons and wild,
bumpy areolae, like relief maps of
Antarctica and Madagascar. I felt
like Vasco da Gama. I hope they're
appreciated now.

INKING ABOUT YOUR BODY

I heard you got an ass tattoo,
as if there were any other kind.

SUSPENDED

I feel like we issued each other
irrevocable make-out licenses, good
anytime, anywhere. It's always a sad
shock to realize this isn't the case.

29
You were too old to be a pothead.

INDEPENDENT WOMEN PART 1
I started listening to Cat Power for you, but screw that—I'm going back to Beyoncé.

BED RINGERS
Being an identical twin does not mean I'm interchangeable with my sister.

I'LL SEND AN SMS TO THE WORLD

I upgraded to unlimited texts for you. Now what?

◆

WITHERING
After you left, all the plants were so distraught they committed suicide.

◆

KEEP IT LIKE A SECRET
I think of you whenever I hear our song playing in a store. I especially think of how you hated all of my music, and how I never even told you it was our song.

SLEEP TIGHT
*You deserved a higher thread count
than I could give you.*

OR FOREVER HOLD MY PEACE
*I'm being compassionately
curious, not snide, when I ask:
Did you fix all that stuff before
you got married? How?*

WOOD PANELING
*I prefer bars designed to resemble
old basement rec rooms, because
they remind me of you and
being young and going wild.*

BACK BURNER

I'm still your plan B, right?

◆

STUNG

I can't believe you're becoming the type of guy who stays cute. Couldn't you have followed Robert Redford instead of Paul Newman—more Sundance, less kid?

◆

ENLIGHTEN UP

I know you love the Power of Now, *but living in the moment does not mean pretending our relationship never happened.*

PERSPECTIVE
No, it's not the end of the world.
But it's the end of a lot.

THE JOSHUA
I finally opened up that restaurant,
and I named a sandwich after you,
like you'd always wanted. Greasy
hair, bug eyes, bad social skills,
and a small penis on rye.

FLAVOR ENHANCER
You appear in all my dreams.
You make the dirty ones
dirtier, and the weird ones
so much weirder.

PICK YOU UP AT ROUTE 7?

Just because we broke up doesn't mean we can't drive from New Jersey to Las Vegas and get impulse-married.

RUBBERNECKED

Every time I drove you home, I prayed for traffic.

MINI GOLF

I miss things we never even got to do together.

SHALL NOT PERISH
FROM THE EARTH

That time we made out while sitting on the Abe Lincoln statue? There should be a statue of that.

GOLDEN YEARS

I really did want to be a grandparent with you. It's just that getting to that point would have been an interminable slog.

THE LINES ARE OPEN

I hereby rescind the prohibition against calling me during Steelers games.

MEAL PLAN

I miss pretending to ignore you in the cafeteria.

PUZZLING

How the hell did our bodies fit together like that, yet we're not together?

NARROWING

I've ruled out academics, the very religious, Europeans, post-hippies, and now, thanks to you, old friends.

ON PHOTOGRAPHY
*Why, in picture after picture,
do we look happier than I ever
remember us being?*

---◆---

YOU-SHAPED SEATING CHART
*Your underwear is the
only thing I remember from
eighth-grade Spanish.*

---◆---

SUFFICIENCY
*I maraschino'd my own cherries,
jerkied my own beef—what other signs
of self-reliance could you want?*

WITLESS PROTECTION PROGRAM
You were adorable and rich,
but you didn't make me laugh.

NUDE FOR NOTHING

Your tepid response
to my naked pictures
means we are never
speaking again.

BEYOND BETTY AND VERONICA
You're the model for all the hot-girl
characters in my comics.

WHAT'S MINE IS YOURS
I thought it was great that we had so much in common. Now I have nothing in my life to enjoy that doesn't remind me of you.

◆

A PRICE ABOVE FAKE RUBIES
Don't forget: A glimpse of your boobs is worth a lot more than a string of Mardi Gras beads.

◆

THE OLD STORY
Boy meets girl. They fall madly in love. It peters out for one of them. You, in this instance.

CLASS OF '76
I wonder how things would have turned out had I gone to the gas station with you after the reunion.

THROWING CATCH PHRASES
If you wanted to do some damage, saying I didn't have enough "wow factor" in bed did the trick.

WAYNE'S MANNERISMS
I'm over you like Batman is over losing his parents.

PRAYER WHEEL
I begged God to let me have you. Then I begged God to free me from you.

SAME-SAME
Dostoevsky said of Russian writers, "We all came out of Gogol's overcoat." And all my ideas about love came out of your jeans.

BUY-BYE
So I fell in love with our broker. Sue me. Oh wait—you did.

GONE GREEN

I'll always be jealous of whoever is with you. And I'm talking all the way to the one pushing you in a wheelchair down the dewy lawn of your old folks' home.

DRESSED TO KILL

Tank tops, on your figure, were truly an implement of war.

POLYGLUT

You spoke six languages. Love wasn't one of them.

CEYLON, FAREWELL

*Sugar: there was never enough
in the tea you made.*

DOOR NUMBER YOU

*I try not to open it
often, but when I do,
that raw, sweet love
for you just waves and
shrugs: "Still here."*

CARVED OUT

*Your wedding announcement is
hidden in my scrapbook, behind a
Mount Rushmore postcard.*

GREEN MONSTER

I miss the jealous rage you used to stoke in me. It was like rocket fuel.

———◆———

WE HAD TO BE NUTS

Only with you did I go on those soaring, crazy carnival rides—the ones where crowds gather to stare and shake their heads, muttering, "They gotta be nuts."

———◆———

HOSED

Though I'm a fireman, I can't put you out.

NEVER STOP PEDALING

My memories of our bike rides are beyond fond. It was when we were on foot that things got rough.

LOCKED OUT

Weird, but in all my mental pictures of you, you're rummaging for your keys.

WONDER WALLS

The book-lined "thinking shed" I built behind the house? It's for thinking about you.

INDOOR VOICES
*Of course I appreciate you trying
to teach me how to argue properly.
I was just a bad student.*

OUTFITTED
*You told me if I dressed better,
I'd have better friends.
Infuriatingly, you were right.*

HI, HONEY

*Coming home to you
never got old. Every day
was like a miracle.*

IN A BIND

Was I reading too much into those long, tight hugs you used to give me?

PRIORITIES
I always thought our spirited breakfast conversations and rollicking walks around the block more than made up for the rote sex.

THREE WINKS MEANS
I'm sad all the codes we formed are now part of a dead language.

BENDER

I'm too old for the Land of Lust by now, but if I could go back and visit for a weekend, I'd take you with me.

ASTRONOMY

My world revolves around you, but I haven't seen you in years. I feel like Pluto, the quasi planet, looking for the sun from a trillion miles away.

LOVE BRIGADE

No fewer than forty sixth-grade boys were in love with you. I am proud of my service in that army.

ST. COUCHINGTON'S WEEKEND
Maybe inventing our own holidays so early in the affair meant we were moving too fast.

ACHE
I mourn the fact that never again will I lift and press you against a wall and kiss you. And even if you let me, my old back wouldn't.

AMOR EMERITUS
Nothing you can do would stop me from loving you. My heart has given you tenure.

PENWOMANSHIP
*I love how your handwriting
stayed loopy and girlish.*

BALLING THINGS UP
*Did you find the surprise I left
in your sock drawer?*

SANDWISH
*We were peanut butter and jelly.
You were the jelly, all slick and
unreliable. I was the peanut butter,
stuck on you.*

STILL A SOLID EDUCATION
*Hey, Reach. I ended up
marrying my safety school.*

HOLDING ON

Dear Old Love,
I still have your . . .

- Princeton sweatshirt. Luckily, it was what I wanted in the first place.

- virginity, but I've taken amazing care of it.

- scent lodged in my nostrils.

- opposition to the word "enthused."

- tradition of leaving white Christmas lights up all year.

- prejudice against raisins.

- third-grade report card, somehow.

- gourd-orange wall-paint. It would take too many coats to cover it up.

- loathin' for words missing their final "g."

- passport. But congratulations on the destination wedding.

- laundry techniques. You domesticated me. In a good way.

- ability to get depressed about not being invited to parties that you would never go to anyway.

- fearlessness about sending back dishes at restaurants.

- errand-based lifestyle.

- folder for our wedding on my desktop.

- baseball autographed by Dwight Gooden. Wanna have a catch?

- pendant. I wear the hideous thing from time to time.

- fondness for, and lascivious pronunciation of, the word "natch."

- Tarot cards. I flip them.

- yoga mat. Some quiet nights I sit on it cross-legged and pretend it's a magic carpet.

- rainbow wristbands. They'll come back, even if you never do.

- sheet music—all the heavy metal classics, arranged for piano.

- custom-molded mouth guard. You'd rather grind your teeth anyway.

SMOKED OUT

Someone else spent a whole night smoking into my hair. I didn't wash it for three days, wishing I could hate that about you again.

HOT WATER

I never got as clean, or as dirty, as I did in the shower with you.

ROLE MODELING

You only compared us to doomed couples. Always Romeo and Juliet; never George and Gracie.

I LOVE YOU ALL

I say "I love you" to people all the time now, to make that time I said it to you mean less.

SHY SIDE

In almost every other aspect of your life you were brutal and commanding, yet you were so vulnerable and sweet when you looked up at me for approval during you-know-what.

ME+U

Why couldn't it have been my initials you carved into that detention-room desk?

STRIDE RITE

You strode with great purpose, but you never had any.

LOW ANGLE
I can still remember how far I have to tilt my head back, and the degree at which I need to fix my gaze to look up at you when we're standing close to each other.

25% OFF
I didn't love you just for your employee discount, but it was definitely part of the equation.

CHEERING SECTION

*You have no idea how hard
I root for you.*

◆

ORIGINS

*I'm embarrassed that my mind works
this way, but whenever I see you with
your kids, I can't help but think of
how much dang fun it must've been
getting you pregnant.*

◆

TOO LEGIT TO QUIT

*I know you worried your
bootyliciousness was on
the wane, but to me it's as
enduring a force as gravity.*

MY ISLAND
Being with you was like being on vacation from the world.

YES, THERE. THERE! LET'S CAMP THERE! YES.

The orgasms were real, but my giddy excitement over all the rugged outdoor activity was fake.

LAST WALTZ
Don't think I quit violin for you. I quit violin for me.

FAR EAST

*I still think you only saw me
as an ethnic studies credit.*

WALK ON THE MILD SIDE

*I'll never forget you saying you
were ready for a "summer of
self-destruction" before spending
two months holding my hand
in city parks.*

ETERNAL RECURRENCE

*The idea of living life over
makes me tired and sad . . .
with the exception of doing
us again.*

ACTION FIGURED

You were the closest thing to a G.I. Joe doll I ever dated—a brave Marine who was totally fake.

MORE CHEESE!

Eating less dairy was your solution for everything. I had the opposite philosophy.

OUCH

I pretended it hurt more than it did so you could feel like a tough guy.

THE DAY THE MUSIC DIED
I know you wrote better songs when we fought. But aren't there enough songs already?

D-BAG
I am very sorry I asked you to douche. I'm sure you smelled fantastic. I was young and didn't know anything.

SEE YOU IN SHUL

So you and I are no more, but the Judaism stuck?

THE PRINGLES OF WISHFUL THINKING

I continue to shop for all your disgusting favorites: instant oatmeal, frozen chicken wings, bacon ranch chips. Just in case.

WASH THAT UPDATE RIGHT OUT OF MY HAIR

The day you changed your Facebook status to "Engaged," I spent 40 minutes in the shower so my boyfriend wouldn't hear me crying.

WE-CUP

I can't bring myself to throw out that ratty old bra of mine you liked so much.

SCREW THAT

I realize I can't fix you. I'll leave that to your husband, since he's the biggest tool I know.

ARRESTED DEVELOPMENT
Your not calling me back was like a network exec who cancels a perfect show too soon.

YON SOLITARY HIGHLAND LASS
I still know all the poems I memorized to impress you.

WINTER

One thing I'll always remember is how we'd clutch each other and laugh when the radiator clanged.

WORKING IT

I still do extra push-ups in your name.

THE OLD CURRENCY

Sexual inflation has radically devalued "I Want to Hold Your Hand." But really, I just want to hold your hand.

YOU ENCRYPT ME
*You'd shake your head when
I couldn't remember passwords.
I've changed them all to something
I can't forget—your name.*

ALL GROWN DOWN

*Maturity was our
great undoing.*

SO LONG, LONG ISLAND
*We'll always have that weekend on
Montauk—the boundless sea, the
boundless fights about your mother.*

HA

I realize now that my patented "tickle torture" was, in fact, torture.

LIKE A MIGHTY OAK

Yours is the only penis I've encountered that I describe as having integrity.

CURSE MY HAZEL EYES

I'm glad you finally found the conservative, blue-eyed, Dutch, Christian Reformed girl of your mother's dreams.

THE ORIGINAL O.D.

I'm going to have to miss your annual overdose this year, as I'll be up North.

INCUBI, SUCCUBI, BYE-BYE

I dream about you so often I fully expect you to show up for my morphine-addled deathbed hallucinations.

PROTOTYPE

How could you stand me? I'm glad you did, but I was such a jerk and poor dresser back then.

BLOWN

You thought I blew it.
I thought you blew it.
The truth is, the people we
eventually married blew it.

DIGITAL FIX

I want to get together and talk
about all the new technologies that
have come out since we parted.

NON-TRANSFERABLE

I still owe you a trip to Venice.
I'm guessing you won't collect,
though I wish you would.

BUSTED

Sometimes I imagine us making out, then stop because I picture your dad catching us. He'd be so pleased that he still has the power to break us apart.

MY SWEET

I bake now! Me! Who couldn't toast bread! Give me your address and I'll send you cookies, cupcakes, brownies . . .

GREAT EXPECTATIONS

I deserve better, but I don't want better.

NOW I KNOW MY ABCs

Thank you for saving the tag from my new bra, after I figured out I was a D-cup instead of a C. You kept it in your wallet, like a much-bragged-about picture of the grandkids. It doesn't make up for the fact that you left me for a girl with As, but still, it was sweet.

BETWEEN EVERYTHING

No one else will sunbathe on the highway median with me.

CARVED IN

Yours is, by far, the deepest and most profound notch on my bedpost.

**DO YOU THINK YOU'RE
WHAT THEY SAY YOU ARE?**
*You were the only one who
could truly appreciate*
Jesus Christ Superstar *with me.*

———◆———

BETTER MAKE IT FIVE
*Just give me three
more chances.*

———◆———

MISSING THE GRADE
*I checked with the registrar at
Harvard—they have no record of
anyone with your name
ever having enrolled.*

YOUR PEE-JAR CAME BETWEEN US
I adored you, but could never have had sex in such a filthy apartment.

TOBOGGAN
Snowfalls, to me, are your body under mine, on a sled, flying.

MFA
For someone with a degree in creative writing, you sure write unoriginal breakup letters.

COMBO
We'll always have the afternoons by your locker.

FIRST CHAIR

I always liked musicians. I just never imagined my favorite would be an aspiring high school band director.

HOUSEKEEPING

I fear we're in for a karmic doozy when I think about what we put hotel maids through.

WHEN LIFE WAS A PIZZA PARTY

Grocery shopping without you is like going to Chuck E. Cheese with no kids.

YOUTH'S A STUFF WILL NOT ENDURE
You had me at my ripest.
I'm glad somebody did.

SAGINAW
I regret that in all our years we never
got to survive a real Michigan winter
together. Coats, snow, body heat,
and holding mitten hands all seem
to be part of some crucial equation,
and we missed it.

PAVLOV'S ASTHMA
Thanks to you,
inhalers turn me on.

IRON, MAN

I don't break easily, so you must be really strong.

ALL SET?
We really can't just play tennis together? My husband—God bless every other aspect of him—is worthless on the court.

LOVE ACTUALLY, ACTUALLY
I enjoyed your chick flicks a lot more than I let on.

HONEST A

Your academic integrity prevented our affair, but I still get turned on when I read about deregulation.

SAINT ME

I want to save the world, just so you can't be the one to do it.

I STILL CARE

You looked better naked than dressed. While there is something secret-weaponish about that, most people will judge you clothed, so please let me give you a makeover.

COMFORTABLY NUMB

*How did you sleep all those nights
with my arm tucked under you?
How did I? I miss those tingling
morning hours, the circulation
creeping back through my veins.*

DROP ME OFF

*Your messy car
felt like home.*

CUSTODY

*You still have my green jacket.
You still have much more
than my green jacket.*

But, Alas . . .

Dear Old Love,
I only regret . . .

- that we turned back before we got to the Grand Canyon.

- haranguing you about wearing jeans too often and dresses not often enough. (Still—wear more dresses!)

- my refusal to accept your leaving with dignity and grace, even if pouting and rage have their own grace.

- comparing you to all those main characters in Billy Joel songs.

- balking on our trip to India.

- having an affair when I didn't even like the other one all that much.

- that I made you turn off the lights that last time.

- portioning out sex like you were a dog in need of treats, even if you were a dog in need of treats.

- not mercy-killing our marriage sooner.

- saying "Don't flatter yourself!" so many times during our breakup.

- not seeing the look on the next sucker's face when he finds out.

- asking you how you got your burn.

- being too timid to do Ecstasy with you. Now I know—you're never too old.

- not enjoying your tantrums while I had the chance.

- we were not sixty years older when we met. Our age difference would seem negligible, plus you would not be able to get away so easily.

- turning you on to yoga, and yoga instructors.

- my last five drunken e-mails.

- not ceding control of the remote more often.

- being able to dish it out but not take it.

- not recognizing how ahead of your time you were.

- never letting you see me cry.

HEALING
*I'm still a little disappointed in me,
and nature itself, for getting over
the loss of you.*

MADE INFORMED

I'm a better man thanks to your bra-unhooking tutorials.

MAKE IT NEW
*Old-fashioned love was
never our style.*

LET'S RUMBLE

I know it got old for you, but I could have gone back and forth hurting each other forever.

HIDDEN ASSETS

I loved that you always fell for tall, ambitious, confident women. Unfortunately, I am none of those things.

GENIE

I keep thinking if I rub this bottle of Maker's Mark vigorously enough, you'll appear.

FORE!

I wasn't amused when you pretended to emboss your testicles with the golf ball personalizer I gave you. Fine, I was amused a little.

BUGGIN'

I put in your initials when I get a high score on Centipede.

BEAMED

Remember at the beach when the moon would always follow us?

HEADING BACK
*Wonder where your ponytail is
swinging now.*

◆

YOU AWAKE?
*I hope you at least appreciate
all the pebbles I flicked at
your window.*

◆

PARENTS, DINNER, MOVIES, KISS

*I like to think ours
was the last proper
date in America.*

WAG

It was puppy love in that we both loved your puppy more than each other.

PEARLY GATE

If there is, as I've been led to believe, an escalator to heaven, I pray I'll be ascending it behind you, with your bum right in front of me.

MILK OF AMNESIA

I couldn't make you young again, or make you forget yourself. My breasts were not, as you and your wizened peers seemed to think, a fountain of youth.

PAIN AS RELIGION
You believed Jesus walked on water, but you wouldn't believe my fibromyalgia was real.

OUT OF ORDER

I should never have described you as "good-looking for a law student."

FOILED
You looked amazing even in your full fencing gear.

SEVEN SISTERLY

Part of me is still waiting for you in the dorm parlor—hair up, clutch in my lap, Lydia practicing the piano in the back.

I NEEDED MY SPACE

I only stayed over every night because of the free parking spot.

PARENT TRAP

My folks liked you a lot better than I did. They have good taste, but it isn't mine.

ABRACADABRA

*How is it you never went down on me
in all that time we were together? I see
it as a kind of post-modern magic act,
like David Blaine suspending himself
in a box over the Thames.*

TRÈS OBVIOUS

*I only called you pretentious
because I wished I was
more like you.*

INTO THIN AIR

*Our ideal vacations couldn't get
along, so neither could we. I had my
Nepal; you had your Cancún.*

THE MIRACLE OF EVERYTHING
You know how when you're young and you first smoke pot, you can't wait to try everything in that enhanced, giddy state? Movies! Hiking! Shopping! I was like that when I got high on you.

DEFACED
That was my head that got cut out of your online dating picture.

SAME BUT DIFFERENT
I melted down my wedding band and had the metal remolded to make a nearly identical ring.

INESCAPE ARTIST

*Even when I dream of you, you
break up with me. Even when it goes
well and we end up making out,
you'll stop, push me away, and say,
"No. This isn't what I want."*

THE HOTLINE IS COLD

*The worst part is,
I can't talk to you about
what to do about you.*

ROCK & ROLLED

*I'll be waiting for you after your
mild fame evaporates.*

I DO WANT WHAT I HAVEN'T GOT

Nothing compares 2 sharing a single pair of headphones with U.

REDRESSING

I want to compensate all those people you've undertipped through the years.

SET, SPIKE

Why couldn't you have taken me as seriously as you took your recreational volleyball league?

A HUNK OF THE PAST

If only it were socially acceptable to have a picture of you in a bathing suit on my desk.

KNOW WHAT I MEAN?

I miss saying, "You know what I mean?" and having you know what I mean.

NEW CELL PLAN

They say every seven years, all our cells are new. There's some contentment knowing that the me who fell in love with you no longer exists.

SOCIAL STUDIES

*I'd know a lot more about the
Roman aqueducts if your seat,
and the perfumed back of your head,
hadn't been right in front of me.*

FIRST PERSON SINGULAR

*"We all miss you" was
a cruel thing to say to
me, and you knew it.*

APPETIZED

*I'm still trying to re-create your
famous twelve-layer nacho dip.*

SHREW'D
*I shouldn't have said those
things about your mother.
Still, I'd say them again.*

ICING
*You may be the last human
who still uses the phrase
"tonsil hockey." And yes, dear,
you were its Wayne Gretzky.*

LONG HOURS, FEW PERKS
*I just wasn't up for being your
assistant micromanager.*

MOHAWKED

Declaring things to be punk rock or not punk rock is definitely not punk rock.

NO DARK SARCASM IN THE KITCHEN
I would gladly let you home-school my kids (as long as you didn't teach them any of the dirty stuff about me).

OUT OF DATE
I still have your mix tape. But I don't have anything to play it on.

PURPOSE-DRIVEN LOVE
*There's no such thing as
a "pointless" affair.*

ADD IT UP
*Songs about moving out. Songs about
standing in the rain. The Violent
Femmes' first album, and Tom Waits.
I only understood music halfways
before you left.*

LOCK
*Please don't cut your hair. I feel
like I own emotional stock in it,
and so should have a vote.*

WOOLLY BULLY

Your hand-knit snowflake sweaters were an implicit promise of hearty masculinity. And you reneged.

ANIME MINE

I could have been everything to you. Except a pigtailed Japanese schoolgirl.

MY UNLUCKY STARS

You got so famous I had to cancel cable.

GOD VS. GOD
*Our religious difference wasn't
the problem, but it's nice to
think that it was.*

SHAKEN
*I couldn't just let you be my
favorite bartender, could I?*

HOME FRIED

*You converted me to
brunch, and now I'm
eating it by myself.*

WHEN HARRY MET TACKY

I like how we had one of those giant wagon wheels for a table in our apartment.

◆

NOT BUSY ENOUGH

I've got a lot going on, but it's still really hard pretending I don't love you.

◆

URINETOWN

You were the first girl to casually pee in front of me.

OM MY

It's hard to meditate because you taught me. You both blazed and blocked my path to peace.

THOREAU JOB

You humored my go-live-in-the-wilderness fantasies more than anyone, including me.

MARY, MARY

I like to think I'm the reason your parents sent you off to an all-girls Catholic school.

COUNTERPOINT

If he had been you, I would have straddled him on the counter and made quick, sweaty work of things. Since he was him, I kissed him twice and headed home.

QUAD PHONICS

If only my old dorm room walls could talk. They'd say, "What are you waiting for? Quit talking about free will and have sex already!"

DEVOUR

We were way too hungry for each other to get married.

ASSUMING I SURVIVE THE INITIAL BLAST

If disaster strikes, I still plan on coming to save you.

◆

NO THERAPY IS MY THERAPY

I treasure the neuroses you bequeathed me. They're all I have left.

◆

HAVE SOME PASSIONS

It was too hard to buy gifts for someone who wasn't addicted to anything. Booze, baseball, old movies—anything!

MY LIFT TICKET
*I've taken up downhill to serve the
memory of your ski-jump nose.*

———◆———

ORDER UP
*They say a good test for how
a man treats humanity is
to watch how he is with
waitresses. I guess that means
you have sex with humanity
between courses.*

———◆———

PATENT EXPIRED
*Is "I might be too drunk to drive,
so can I stay the night?" still your
signature move?*

STUD POKER

I even miss your gambling addiction,
how to you losing big was just as
fun as winning big.

LIKE A SURGEON

You were brilliant at
breaking up—decisive and
compassionate, giving me a
little hope, but not too much.
I'm grateful.

REVIEWING MY BOOKS

I could've been more generous—
bed-wise, if not financially.

REPURPOSING

I wish I had a piece of the purple carpet that was in your bedroom when we were together. I'd make it into a scratching post.

KIND OF BLUE

Like how one righteous person can save a city, your affection for Miles Davis, and the fact that he was a soundtrack for our first night together, keeps me from writing off all jazz.

FADE

For months you were all I thought about, and now I can't remember your name.

VISCERAL

I would skin a donkey for ten more minutes of your unwavering affection.

OCTOBER 21

I hate that I can't forget your birthday.

THAT'S RICH

The truly wealthy don't go bragging about it. It's why I never talked you up.

DISTANT EARLY WARNING

Dear Old Love,
As if I'd never noticed . . .

- how quickly you cleaned up afterward.

- that the "Tax Info" tab on your computer was a link to a premium Australian nudie site.

- the way you kissed your male friends good-bye.

- how you only looked at you when we did it in front of the mirror.

- you only called me back on Fridays, at 4 P.M.

- your secret closet of hair-growth formulas.

- your secret closet of hair-removal formulas.

- what you were doing under the covers.

- that you always took the bigger slice.

- the solar system tattoo was a cover-up.

- the slight hesitation. Every time.

- how even my cockatiel was wary around you.

- little slices of condom wrapper on your floor, a decreasing volume of Astroglide, and an increase in your tendency to call me "Tim."

- all the men in your family have women's butts. I had to get out before the hammer came down.

- that you often erased your call history.

- that we both have hands that look way older than they should.

- you wanted a diamond and not my Grandma's old-ass ruby.

- your forced joviality around kids.

- that despite your supposed love of wine, you couldn't even tell if a bottle was corked.

- how much work you put into your "regular guy" jeans.

- the amounts you dropped into beggars' cups.

- that you were incapable of a full-body smile.

BEHIND DREAMS
You said, "I dreamt we had anal sex."
I said, "That's interesting."
Let me know if, all these years later,
that dream recurs . . .

I HOPE IT *DOES* WORK!
That time I said I hoped it didn't
work out with your new guy?
I didn't mean it.

MISO LOST

I'm afraid to order sushi without you.

NO AIR KISSES, EITHER

Please tell your new wife she really shouldn't hug me when she sees me on the street.

FLICK

I still find myself buying Vietnam-era Zippo lighters for your collection.

MY NINJA

I insisted that you keep your socks on not because your feet felt cold against mine, but because I didn't want to see your ankle tattoo of a cartoon turtle.

MY CHEMICAL ROMANCE

You looked and talked right, but the smell was wrong.

NICE EVERYTHING

You were great at complimenting my eyes. Always with the eyes. But I needed to be lathered in compliments, mind and body.

FAULT

I don't blame you. Well, I do, but maybe if I say it enough, I'll believe it.

AW, FRESCO
We never got around to using that fancy picnic basket, did we?

———◆———

OEDIPUS NEXT
Dating you made me feel like the single mother of a 30-year-old.

———◆———

RAINED IN
I've gotten over my misguided stance against umbrellas. I now own several so large they make everyone on the sidewalk hate me. If you come back, I promise to keep you dry.

ON MUTE

You were so quiet. I'm still not sure if you were having a good time.

IN THE TEETH

Now that you're in a band you don't give me credit for being the one who talked you out of dental school.

YOU'RE RUBBERS, I'M GLUE

That bowl of condoms at your bedside was as intimidating as it was enchanting.

PEAKED

After you, it's all been anticlimax.

TOO LATE
Okay, okay, I'll dance with you.

CO-EDUCATION
To me, you're forever wrapped up in Kant, darts, and collegiate pubbery.

ASHES TO ASHES
Will you at least deliver my eulogy?

SPLOTCH

If only I'd been a better and less abstract painter, I'd have a more realistic record of what you look like naked. "Capture your soul." What was I thinking?

UNPERSUASIVE

I tried so hard to talk myself into you.

ON THROWING ME A BONE

Pity sex from you was better than true-love-forever sex with just about anyone else.

TRICKY DICK

Your penis has a leftward bend in it; your politics bend to the right. Only one is responsible for why we couldn't be together.

SHROUD OF YOUR-IN

Whenever I see a fur-trimmed hood pulled way up, I can't help but hope that it's your face nestled inside.

WHAT A CROCKETT

I thought your stubble would scour away all my rough spots.

OOPS

We were so in love we forgot we weren't supposed to be.

RIGHT A POUT NOW
If only your heart had been as full as your lips.

I'VE GOT SPIRIT, YES I DO
You can take the girl out of the cheerleading uniform, but you can't take the fervid desire for that girl out of me.

FOOTBALL BEDSPREAD

When I first walked into your room,
it reminded me of my little brother.
I should've run for cover, but instead
I curled up and stayed.

MISMATCH

The sex was incredible. You were unbearable.

TEEING OFF

If you own more T-shirts with dick
jokes printed on them than not,
you might want to rethink your
wardrobe's relationship to dick jokes.

SUCKY
*When I described you as vampiric,
it was meant as a compliment.*

THE LAST GENTLEMAN
*You were so chivalrous. Now, I expect
other men to be the same, and I am
disappointed every time.*

JUST WISHES
*Happy birthday.
Also, screw you.
Also, call me. Please?*

B'GOSH
*Because of you, overalls, to me,
are forever the height of style.*

FIZZED OUT
*I Googled you hoping to find
a sordid police report, but
all I found was information
about your antique
soda-can collection.*

MORE THAN ENOUGH
*It's not that you were even that
amazing. You were just you.*

PRIMARY CARE
*I never thought we were playing
doctor. I believed you could heal me.*

APOLOGY BLANKET
*Assume I'm aware
of all the things I did
wrong, and that I'm
sorry I did them.*

GAMES MEN PLAY
*I miss trying to out-alpha
your boisterous father.*

BUILT FOR ONE, USED FOR TWO
*You had me at
"get on the handlebars."*

OLIVE GARDENING
*Not that it makes any
difference, but I saw your
"ancestral" family lasagna
recipe on the back of a
Ronzoni box.*

FREDDY'S COMING FOR YOU
*It's time for you to get out of my
life now. My boyfriend has begun
to have dreams about you, and
it's creeping both of us out.*

COURTLY LOVE

If love is a food court, you gave me a sample of bourbon chicken on a toothpick. What I really wanted was a hot pretzel, the teriyaki lunch special, frozen yogurt, and a giant cinnamon roll. Plus a pound of Gummi Worms for the ride home.

NAMELESS DREAD

I'm still afraid of you, even if I can't quite remember why.

BEDDING THE RULES

I suffer fools gladly, but only in the sack.

DRAWN OUT

I'll never draw elaborate cartoon postcards for anyone else. It's hard to believe I ever did that. I don't just miss you—I miss me.

NOT NOW

I want you then.

HUNGRY EYES

True, there is no law against looking, but you didn't have to proclaim it with such frequency and vigor.

COST OF DOING BUSINESS

*I had to screw, and therefore lose,
several close friends to get over you.*

EVERYONE SAYS I PIE YOU

*I learned the tough way you can't
say "I love you" just with pies.*

ALIEN LANES

*Perhaps on your home planet
The Dead Mackerel Position
is the most tender and
affectionate of the ways your
people make love.*

RUG RATTED

I shouldn't have let your kids scare me off. But they were scary!

BIG BAND BY THE SEA

Even in this retirement village, I can't retire thoughts of waltzing with you.

FANCY MEETING YOU HERE

One more "coincidence" and I call the police.

PERSPECTIVE

That woman walking her dog who saw us having sex in the park that night? She has better memories of our relationship than I do.

CUE KISS

I pray we have our "You had a crush on me? I had a crush on you!" moment.

CLASS DISMISSED

I was pretty sure breaking up was the right thing to do. I'm even more confident now that I saw you're online calling yourself "The Professor."

I'M NO SLOUCH

You may not have intended this, but your posture felt like a rebuke to my entire way of life.

GRADUATION

Thank you for ruining the sexy schoolgirl look for me. I'm not being sarcastic—I'm genuinely grateful.

GHOSTED

If I have to be haunted by someone, I'm glad it's you.

A STRETCH
Watching you spontaneously strike yoga poses on the sidewalk brought me close to Nirvana.

THE WAY I SEE IT
Whenever anyone meets you, they always call me and say, "Him? Really? That's who you've been obsessed with all these years? I don't believe it. Him?" And I'll feel awful, because what more could you want than a person who sees the greatness in you that is invisible to the rest of the world?

TOUR DE PANTS
I've mounted your old bike seat on my wall like some exotic fertility symbol.

HISTORY REPEATING

*You are the reason I broke up
with my last boyfriend,
and the reason I'll break up
with my next.*

HOW POETRY GETS MADE

*You cared more about your
rhapsodic odes to my beauty
than you did about me.*

THOSE FOUR LITTLE WORDS

*I know you thought it was
funny when I said, "I love you,"
and you replied, "I love me, too."
But it wasn't.*

OFF TRACK

I don't blame you for any of it. My train was liable to crash at any moment, and you just happened to be on it at the time.

MONEY IN THE MIDDLE

Me, you, and your bank account turned out to be the least sexy threesome. Did it have to be on top every time?

YOU'RE JUST NOT THAT INTO ME

I never leave the bookstore without checking for you in the relationship aisle first.

ALARMING

I finally found someone who doesn't mind if I wake them up in the morning to say good-bye.

MY KINDA CONTRADICTION
I like how your computer keyboard was always covered with a protective film, but you hated condoms.

LONG TERM
But I had already looked into booking us adjacent grave sites!

EXPOSED

*A current snapshot of you erased
25 years of fantasizing about
what could have been.*

SCHEME

*I know I'm supposed
to say, "Falling in love
with you was never
part of the plan."
But it was.*

AWAY FROM IT ALL

*My "happy place" is our country
house, never to be built.*

FOGHEART

If it's a choice between going senile and allowing my muddled brain to think we ended up together, or easing gracefully into old age with all my faculties intact . . . I'm torn.

TRAVELED FAR

I feel your spirit in unexpectedly cool breezes that seem to come from other seasons, other continents, other centuries.

BEYOND HUGGER

Sometimes, when I'm walking past a tree, I'll think of you and want to make out with it.

REUNION TOUR?

Even The Specials got back together. Call me if you're feeling washed up.

OFFLINE

While you were busy searching for missed connections online, you missed one with me.

ONE MORE NIGHT

When anyone asks if I'd prefer a one-night stand or a fling with an ex, I'm thinking about you when I say a fling with an ex.

A GIFT

I finally fixed up my life, but, if you must know, I did it only so you can have something to mess up again.

WEIGHT FOR ME

You didn't break my heart—you just made it heavier.

CULTURAL RELATIVISM

In some societies, the way I eat noodles—inhaling them in one giant cylinder—is considered a compliment to the chef, not grounds for ball-busting.

JUNIOR HIGH POINT

*Thank you for teaching me that I was,
at 13, worth dancing with.*

GIDDY UP

*Thoughts of you do to
me what dreams of
horses do for little girls.*

FOUNDATION

*If I had known I was going to meet
the woman you would leave me
for when we stopped at your office,
I would have put on makeup.*

NOTES FOR A COUNTRY SONG
*You're no good, but I'm going to be
pissed when you marry someone else.*

◆

GOING COMPARTMENTAL
*I was so outraged when you
slept with someone else that I
momentarily forgot I had been
cheating on you for months.*

◆

RAMBLE ON
*You read The Hobbit to me
in our bed-fort at night.
Mostly I remember how nice
your voice was.*

OUT OF CONTROL
I usually like to be the one in control, but oh man, did I love being pinned under you.

SAME BUT DIFF

I'm so miserable without you, it's like you're still here.

COMFORTABLY UNCOMFORTABLE
What I wouldn't give to feel that awkward around you again.

BLATHER, RINSE, REPEAT
*Every five years or so I contact you.
Then I learn my lesson. Then I contact
you again five years later.*

———◆———

ABSENCE IS A PRESENCE
*I miss you in ways that are
shocking and unproductive.*

———◆———

NOT QUITE A REGRET
*On one hand, I should have
kissed you. On the other hand,
I've had thirty good years
imagining that kiss.*

THE DEAR OLD LOVE
FILL-INS

It can be tough to come up with a sentence or two that concentrates the essence of a relationship. To make things easier for you, we've provided a head start with a series of Universal Love Experiences; you just fill in the relevant details. Then post them on your blog, line the birdcage with them, or tie them to a bunch of balloons and let them float away.

Not a _____ goes by that I don't
_____ the fact that we never
got a chance to _____.

When I see you on the _____,
it's all I can do not to _____
my _____ until it _____.

At breakfast, do you still stir _____
into your _____? I always found
that _____.

I can't help but remember how your
_____ looked in the neon light
of the _____. I just wish I'd taken
a _____ of it!

On the surface, our first big fight was about
who forgot to _____, but I
think it was really about which of us
_____ the other more.

I wonder if we'd still be together if I had just admitted I was a _____, instead of saying you had a _____ so big it blocked out the _____.

When I have to wait in a long _____, I think about your amazing _____, and time moves faster.

That time we were _____ along the _____ overlooking the _____, and you said you'd _____ me forever—you didn't mean it, did you?

I sometimes say your name while I'm

_____ on the _____.

Very quietly, so only the _____

can hear it.

I regret not having the _____

to ask you to let me _____

your _____.

You are the only person I've ever _____

whose _____ smelled like ripe

_____.

Do you remember the time we _____
on top of the _____? And the
moon looked like a _____? I don't.

You were my first _____,
but I was too _____ to
ever _____ you.

I consider the real moment of my birth to
be that day in Mr./Ms. _____'s
_____ class when you _____
me your _____.

I saved every _____ you ever
_____ me. When I see them,
I _____.

Whenever I'm in a crowded _____,
I think I see your _____.

I'll dream that we meet up and _____.
Just _____. And I wake up
_____ing. Every time.

You gave me the best _____
of my _____.

Every night at midnight, I fight the urge to

_____ you.

I'll never _____ anyone as much

as I _____ you. No one should

_____ another human being that

much. It's not healthy!

I hope you're _____.

ACKNOWLEDGMENTS

Thanks to everyone who has sent in a Dear Old Love note. This would not exist without you. I also thank all the dear old loves. No grudges! No regrets!

I want to give credit to Kelly Ambrose, as this book is shot through with his comic brilliance.

The entire team at Workman Publishing has been great—smart, professional, and kind. There, I especially appreciate Natalie Rinn, who plucked Dear Old Love from the blogosphere and nudged it in all the right directions.

This project got a huge boost from good friend and agent Devin McIntyre at Mary Evans Inc. And I'm grateful to my wife, Izzy Grinspan, for her support, companionship, and knack for coming up with ingenious headlines.

ABOUT THE AUTHOR

Andy Selsberg has written for *The Onion*, *GQ*, *The Oxford American*, *The Believer*, Salon.com, and other publications. He is also an adjunct lecturer in English at John Jay College, CUNY, and a former stand-up comedian. He lives in Brooklyn, New York, and his website is www.dearoldlove.com.